NEW
BEGINNING

STEPHANIE
DOWRICK

PENGUIN BOOKS

Penguin Books Australia Ltd
250 Camberwell Road, Camberwell, Victoria 3124, Australia
Penguin Books Ltd
80 Strand, London WC2R 0RL, England
Penguin Putnam Inc.
375 Hudson Street, New York, New York 10014, USA
Penguin Books, a division of Pearson Canada
10 Alcorn Avenue, Toronto, Ontario, Canada M4V 3B2
Penguin Books (NZ) Ltd
Cnr Rosedale and Airborne Roads, Albany, Auckland, New Zealand
Penguin Books (South Africa) (Pty) Ltd
24 Sturdee Avenue, Rosebank, Johannesburg 2196, South Africa
Penguin Books India (P) Ltd
11, Community Centre, Panchsheel Park, New Delhi 110 017, India

First published by Penguin Books Australia 2001
This paperback edition published 2002

1 3 5 7 9 10 8 6 4 2

Cover design by Melissa Fraser, Penguin Design Studio
Text Design by Sandy Cull, Penguin Design Studio
Cover and internal photography by Lynette Zeeng
Typeset in 11/12 Goudy by Post Pre-Press Group, Brisbane, Queensland
Printed and bound in Australia by McPherson's Printing Group
Maryborough, Victoria

National Library of Australia
Cataloguing-in-Publication data:

Dowrick, Stephanie.
Every day a new beginning.

ISBN 0 14 300104 3.

1. Love. 2. Interpersonal relations.
3. Self-actualization (Psychology). I. Title.

158.1

www.penguin.com.au

For my beautiful daughter, Kezia

Special thanks to Julie Gibbs, Lesley Dunt, Sandy
Cull and Amanda Toombs at Penguin Australia:
my wonderful, wonderful 'team'.

Encouragement expresses a 'big heart' –
and the joy in living that goes with it.
Your power to encourage yourself and others
can literally transform your life.
It opens your eyes to your own strengths.
It allows you to ask less of others – and
receive more.
It supports you to move on from
disappointment and recover from loss.
It gives you the courage to try something
different.
It restores hope.
The habits and practices of encouragement
are easily learned.

Every day . . . is a new beginning.

Waking, set your inner
compass.
Evoke the quality that
you need (patience,
courage, trust, good
humour, resilience,
forgiveness).
Think of that quality
often through your day.
Let it inspire you.

A sense of abundance arises with
the phrase 'I can afford to . . .'
'I can afford to be generous
(tolerant, cheerful, forgiving,
trusting).'

Value your own existence.
Others will take their cues from
your inner attitude.

Speak about *what's going well.*
Just that small change can
dramatically shift the atmosphere
around you.

Recognise which of your
behaviours bring you closer to
people and which push them away.
Adjust accordingly.

Blaming others *always* drains
your power.
Accepting your part in things
gives you an invaluable
opportunity to make them better.

Your life blossoms when you can switch from fearing the worst to expecting the best.
Assume the best always.
Be confident that you can bear the occasional disappointment.

Talk to yourself
encouragingly.
The person who can
learn from setbacks is
always a winner.

What happens to you eventually
matters less than how you describe
it to yourself.
Interpret events positively.
Not 'He's late because I don't
matter', but 'He's late because he
has a lot on.'
Not 'Nothing good ever happens
to me', but 'It didn't work so well
this time. What else can I try?'

We are rarely 'ready' to meet a
significant challenge.
The strengths we long for arise
as and when they are needed –
not before.

Meet your fears with compassion,
not self-hatred or scorn.
Fear is part of life.
It is in the face of fear that you
discover courage and resilience.

Often something troublesome in our lives needs nothing more than a brief time of close attention. Set those feelings of being overwhelmed to one side and ask, 'What's needed here?'

Taking the time to know yourself
is not selfish.
It isn't possible to know other
people intimately without
also feeling at home
with yourself.

Seek out what will
inspire you.
A life without inspiration
is a half-life only.

Look at the big picture when
thinking about disappointments.
Put them alongside whatever's
gone well.
The more inclusive your point
of view, the less easily you
will feel overwhelmed.

Make room for happiness.
Treasure kindnesses.
Let slights go.

Never hold back
a kind word.

Discover the difference between
doing what might impress others
and doing what brings you joy.

Free yourself to do your best
without needing to be the best.

Read the language of your body.
Notice when you feel most alive.
Do more of that.

Self-pity drains love.
Pitying yourself, you invite others
to pity you also.
Sometimes they will feel irritated
or angry.
Gather your powers
of self-encouragement.
Invite encouragement and
confidence from other people also.

Find what's positive when you
look in the mirror.
You may be tempted to focus on
flaws. (A cosmetic industry
depends on this.)
Look more closely.
See what's pleasing.
Good health, ease of movement,
sensuality, features you
secretly admire!
Nothing will train you better in the
invaluable skill of 'looking wisely'.

Improve your looks from
the inside out.
Anyone who loves life
is irresistible.

Be curious about your
inconsistencies.
We all have them.
The moments that 'take you by
surprise' also take you to new
levels of self-knowledge.

Be kind to yourself.
It makes it so easy then to
be kind to other people.

Spring-clean your attitudes.
Toss out those that are dated
or unattractive.
Make room for kindness.

The rules for kindness are simple.
Listen with your mind.
Speak from your heart.
Be open, direct, encouraging.
Believe in your capacity to affect
others positively.

Take time to connect with
someone who's speaking to you.
Look at the person.
Hold their gaze.
Connect to them with all
your senses.
That brings you quickly into
their world.
It reassures them. It centres you.

Everyone loves to be encouraged,
including the people you believe
'don't need it'.
Encourage your boss, parents and
heroes, as well as those who
seem to have less power than
you do.

The most perfect form of
encouragement is the response
that tells the other person that
you care.

Your grandmother was right.
If you don't have something kind
to say, say nothing at all.
If envy, bitterness, self-pity or
anger get in your way, deal
with them.
Limit the problems you create
for other people.

It's easy to see suffering
a mile off.
Check that you can see
happiness just as clearly.

Create the best possible
conditions for happiness.
Weed out negativity.
Silence criticisms.
Don't threaten, cajole,
whine or bribe.
Speak warmly, appreciatively.
Rejoice in the outcome.

Want to be liked more?
Think and speak positively.
Cultivate a wide variety
of interests.
Enjoy your own company.
Accept people as they are.
Enjoy *life*.

Treasure the power you
have to influence other
people positively.
It's the greatest power you
will ever have.

Speak to the best that's in
everyone.
Usually they will respond from
the same place.

Encouraging others becomes easy
when you realise how exquisitely
interdependent all of our
lives are.

Don't leave yourself out
when thinking
about love.
Love joins you to others.
It also joins you to the
deepest parts of yourself.

Let experience teach you quickly
what is worth struggling for
and what is not.

Know what your strengths and
talents are.
You can't begin to make good
use of them until you
recognise them.

44

False modesty undermines
your power.
Step over it.

Many things won't go your way.
Celebrate extravagantly when
they do!

Re-enchant your life.
Look at one thing each day
with wonder.
Really see it: a tiny mountain of
salt; how yellow the butter is;
the smile of welcome on
a friend's face;
pink across an evening sky.

Small rituals invite you to notice
what you might otherwise rush by.
Give thanks before you eat.
Eat by candlelight.
Celebrate birthdays with an
invitation to share photos,
memories, stories.
Mark each end of the day with
quiet reflection.
Send the people you care for an
inspirational verse by e-mail on
the first day of the month.
Greet the seasons with a shared
walk in nature.
Slow down and see what you have.

Value your instinct for beauty.
Take time to look deeply into
whatever nourishes you.
Create small touches of beauty
wherever you are.

Behave with great respect
towards yourself.
Be unafraid to say 'No' to
anyone who asks something of you
that feels wrong.

Say 'No' confidently.
You don't ever need to do
something wrong to make
someone else feel all right.
Your life also matters.

Expect respect and
kindness.
Where they are absent,
walk away.

Give respect and kindness – always.
This steadies you. And lifts
your spirits.

Find out how possible it is to
admit you have been wrong,
without loss or shame.

As soon as you catch yourself
being critical, bitter or
undermining, *stop it*.
Negativity is a habit. Unpractised,
it falls away.

The air is never 'cleared' by
pointing out someone else's faults.
The air is cleared when you can
let go of *your irritations*.

Keep things simple.
Use love as your reference point.
'Is this encouraging?'
'Is this kind?'

Observe the effect you have
on other people.
If your behaviour hurts or
discourages them, make amends.

The right amount of guilt is
extremely useful.
Too much – you drown in self-pity.
Too little – you become
dangerously inured to the pain
of others.
The right amount frees you to feel
sorrow, make amends, learn
lessons and reconnect.

On the days you feel powerless,
be especially vigilant about how
you are affecting others.
Never say that 'nothing is wrong'
when you are breathing fire and
wrapped in a black cloud.

Value your sensuality.
Even in grim times it is
still possible to enjoy
tastes, touch, sounds,
sights.

The equation is simple.
The better we behave towards
others, the better we feel ourselves.
Take every opportunity to
be generous.

Be utterly consistent in the way you treat other people.
Nothing can steady you more effectively.

Never label other people.
It cuts you off from their
humanity – and your own.

Sometimes we see only the good
in others.
Then we see only the bad.
The truth is, people are far more
complex than either good
or bad.

Take it for granted that you will
never fully know another person.
Remain open, interested,
willing to shift and expand
your awareness.

When someone is driving you
nuts ask yourself, 'What's going
on with me today?'
Other people's annoying habits
can be the most telling barometer
of our own internal state.

Be a 'wise warrior' when you have
to face a difficult situation.
Feet pressing into the ground.
Knees slightly bent.
Breathe from your belly. Breath
bringing you to your centre.
Alert. Balanced. Confident.

When feelings of worthlessness
arise, meet them calmly.
'My life has value; no more but no
less either than that of any other
human being.
My *life has value*.'
Let worthlessness drift away.

Be kind without asking
who deserves it.
Doing that, you truly
discover the taste
of freedom.

Remain aware of other
people's dignity.
Often nothing more is needed
to lift your communication to
its highest level.

If you love someone, let love
guide your behaviour.
Remembering love makes it
easy not to respond to every
petty irritation.

Someone speaks rudely to you?
Take it for granted that their
rudeness has *nothing to do with you.*
Assume it reflects their bad day.
Respond courteously.

Someone is *routinely* rude or
disappointing?
Speak up. Let them know that
you are uncomfortable.
Ask *them* to suggest a workable
solution.

Because you assume something doesn't always mean that it's true. Give other people the chance to put your mind at rest.

It's easy to be pleasant and gracious when things go our way. The challenge of maturity is to be pleasant and gracious when things do *not* go our way.

Cutting other people down never
builds you up.
Personal power flows from your
choice to be thoughtful –
whatever the circumstances.

Cultivate your highest
ideals.
Talk about them.
Read and write
about them.
Praise them in others.
Live them out.

My highest ideal is compassion.
Am I always compassionate?
No, I am not.
Nevertheless, I allow compassion
to light my path.
And when I lift my gaze, that light
is *always* burning.

Create a small altar in your home.
Place photographs on it of the
people who inspire you.
Leave sacred texts there.
And fresh flowers.
Light incense or a candle.
Respect those outward signs
of your inward journey.

All will be well.
Use this as your mantra:
All will be well.
Experience infinite stability
beyond the chaos.

Love your life.
Do what makes your heart sing.
Learn something new that
stimulates you. Or gives
you peace.
Spend time with people who
lift your spirits.

Reflect on how the air
itself changes when
someone uplifting comes
into a room.
Be that person.

Take the time and interest needed
to understand other people.
Listen to their stories.
It will transform the way you
behave towards them.

You 'can't help' thinking about
something disappointing, grim
or hurtful?
Think about it *more intensely*,
not less.
Write down your concern and
describe the feelings that go
with it.
Ask yourself, 'What would help?'
Or 'What do I need to
understand here?'

There isn't a solution for every problem.
Some problems have to be survived. Nothing more.

Balance personal growth with social awareness.
It opens your life out wonderfully.
It saves you from loneliness.

Living as a loving person
does not mean loving everyone
in the same way.
It simply means being thoughtful
and respectful whomever you
are with.
Respecting boundaries and
difference is part of that.

Give more to your loved ones
than is needed.

Enter fully into the relationships that
you value.
Let yourself be wholly present.

Let your friends know that you value them.
Turn to them as often with good news as with bad.
Speak to them openly about how they enhance your life.
Be encouraging and hopeful on their behalf as well as your own.

If you have something to resolve
with another person,
sit side by side.
Speak collaboratively: 'How are
we going to sort this out?'
Remind each other, 'Our best
chance is to work on this
together.'
Discover how this deepens your
connection. And how good
'win–win' feels.

Gratitude is the most powerful remedy against self-pity and irritation.
Take every chance to say, 'Thank you.'

Praise lavishly.
The people around you
will flourish.
Your world will *glow*.

The useful question is not 'Am I
loving enough?'
It is 'Are my *actions* loving?'
Loving words that are not backed
up by loving actions are worthless.

Keep a close watch on who is
giving and who is taking in any
close relationship.
Who is demanding – who is
conceding.
Who is setting the rules – who
must follow them.
Search constantly for the high
ground where each person gives
and gets.

Don't use encouragement as an excuse to tell someone what they ought to be feeling.
People may need to express their pain and have it accepted *before* they can move on.
Temper encouragement with empathy and respect.

It is not a failure of
self-encouragement
to feel sad.
Sadness is appropriate in
many situations.
Sadness can also be a useful
invitation to look into a complex
situation more deeply.

The difficult situations give us
an unparalleled chance to grow.
You don't need to seek them out;
they will find you.
Rise up to meet them.

Angry people are skilled at
noticing what's wrong.
Be just as skilled at noticing
what's pleasing.

Give yourself a break.
It helps others to breathe
much more easily.

Never underestimate your power
to hurt other people.
Regard it like dynamite. Handle
it just as carefully.

It *is* possible to surrender anger.
Speak to yourself soothingly.
Interpret events positively.
Deflect the triggers for frustration.
Avoid alcohol or drugs.
Release strong feelings through
physical work or exercise.
Learn to meditate and to relax.
Let the wind blow through
your hair.

Love cannot coexist with the
desire to hurt someone.
Wish them well. Do your best.
Or walk away.

If you have something important to say, say it when you are genuinely free of anger.

Anger can cut us off from the
connections we long for.
You begin to leave loneliness
behind when you can ask, 'What
would help here?'

Trust gives freedom. It doesn't
take it away.
You demonstrate your love by
showing others that you
trust them.

If you dishonour someone's
trust, *apologise*.
Learn from the experience.
Make reparations.
Move on.

There are some hurts that you
won't get over.
But you can get *on*, nevertheless.
Recognising what you have
learned helps.
So does understanding how
universal suffering is.
Observe, too, that life continues
to give – even while it takes.

Return persistently to whatever
supports you (prayer, meditation,
bushwalks, music, friends, reading,
writing in your journal).
Use that support in good times as
well as bad.

Train yourself to *take in what is going well.*
And to view the rest with wise detachment.

Think lovingly.
And sometimes let your mind rest.
There is great loneliness in a
life where you are too busy for
other people.
And great sadness when you are
too busy for yourself.

Nominate many days as feasts
of thanksgiving.
Telephone a friend.
Write a letter of thanks to
a mentor.
Send flowers to someone who
needs cheering.
Give time or money to a stranger.

Self-reliance is admirable.
Recognising what other
people contribute to your
happiness is priceless.

We glimpse the inner world of
someone else through listening.
Open your mind and heart.

You need to quieten your mind
to listen well.
Set your theories, responses and
anecdotes aside.
Be fully present.

If you say, 'I don't have time right now', then make time quickly.

Life is full of repetitive tasks.
Your resentment makes no
difference to the task. Only to
the way you feel.
Let resentment go.
Your tension will go also.

Banish slave words from
your vocabulary.
Should. Must. Ought. Have to.
Choose to do what needs to
be done.

Try a new response in a stuck situation.

Notice when it is *not* your turn
to do something.
Do it.
What freedom!

Limit the frustration too much
choice can cause.
Know which choices are worth
your time and which are not.
Often you are choosing between
two equally fine possibilities.
Choose. Act. Enjoy.

Know what your strengths are.
Recognise what brings you joy.
See how you affect others.
*Use that self-knowledge when
making big decisions.*

You will resent less when you
also rush less.
Cut your list of 'have to' jobs
in half.
(And in half again?)

Your mind works best when you
feed it well.
Take 'mind fitness' seriously.
Learn new things. Read widely.
Discuss complex topics.
Take risks. *Engage*.

Use your non-dominant hand.
Develop your creativity.
Take chances.
Breathe deeply. Eat with gratitude
and pleasure. Drink lots of water.
Make friends and value them.
Give and receive love.
*This is a recipe for a long and
happy life.*

Our lives need order.
Give your days a rhythm and shape.
Balance work with rest; rest with
stimulation; what is new with
what's familiar.
Value what matters over
what clamours.
Do what matters first.

It's possible to welcome
interruptions and changes of plan
when you generally feel in charge
of your diary and your life.

Use your imagination to create
moments of respite.
Take yourself somewhere beautiful in
your mind.
Breathe in that beauty.
Breathe out – and feel refreshed.

Behave as though you have all the
time in the world.
And still leave nothing undone
that's truly important.

It is so tempting to believe that
your happiness depends on other
people's decisions.
(I will be happy if I get this
job/this award/this recognition.)
But that gives away too much of
your power.
Success is arbitrary and often
unfair. Detach a little from it.
Your own life is a gift.
Your value lies within.
No one can take that from you.

Know how to close a door inside
your mind when you go home
from work.
Visualise your work in a closed
drawer where you can't reach
it until the next day.
Be present to the world that
exists outside your work.

Setting perfectionism aside, you will work faster, make fewer mistakes and have greater insight.
Risk it.

Often a sense of restlessness,
futility or hopelessness directly
precedes new insights.
Persist.
Trust that after a dark night
the new dawn is
especially precious.

See a bad day for what it is:
a bad day.
It is no more a predictor of the
rest of your life than your last
great day was.
Good days. Bad days. They come.
And they go.

Use tough situations to practise soothing yourself down rather than working yourself up.

Change a low mood by 'acting as if' (*as if* you are optimistic, interested, wholehearted et cetera).
A low mood is only ever part of who you are.
Move beyond it, trusting your greater self.

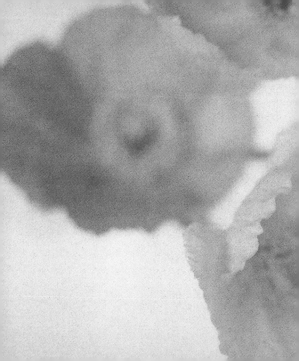

Make time for stillness.
Five minutes at either end of the
day can bring you balance.
Take time, too, to read a simple
verse or a few lines from a
great teaching.
The effect can be as dramatic
as watering a plant that has
been parched.

Discover the fullness of silence.
Experience peace.

Know that breathing out
is just as important as
breathing in.
Let tension go.

Use your own breath to give
you space.
Breathe slowly in and out *before*
you respond to something
that's important.

Recognise that your own
experiences and reflections are an
invaluable source of wisdom.
Use books, courses and teachers of
all kinds.
But also value what your own life
has taught you.

Treasure what you have
already learned.
You may not need to
learn it twice.

Don't ask, 'Why me?'
Ask, 'How can I best move
through this?'

Be cautious about talking too
much too soon.
Find out what you yourself
know before you ask, 'What do
you think?'

It's fine to substitute hope
for experience.
But sometimes it is also useful
to ask, 'Have I been
here before?'

Be unafraid to hope on behalf
of others.
But take care that your hopes for
them are not a burden.

Stay away from people who can
harm you – even in your thoughts.
Think often and with gratitude
about the people who love you
or inspire you.
Limit the thinking time you give
to people who have hurt or
disappointed you.

Sometimes we are afraid to admit
to what we most want.
Treat those fears tenderly.
But don't let them hold
you back.

Hang around people who love life.
Sniff their armpits. Repeat
their jokes.
Live in their skin for a while.
Get it.

There is no victory in
doing down someone
you love.
Love lifts you – and
allows you to lift
others also.

If someone says with genuine feeling, 'I'm sorry. Will you forgive me?', the answer is always 'Yes!'

Should you give someone you care
about 'another chance'?
Absolutely!
We can all act foolishly.
This means only that we still
belong to the human race.

Love the people in your life with
your eyes open.
Let them know that *they do
not need to be perfect* to have
your love.

Don't worry that your
imperfections will 'give you away'.
Your imperfections allow other
people to feel at home with you.

You become truly part of the world when you recognise how its contradictions and its beauty live in you.

STEPHANIE DOWRICK is the author of a number of much-loved international bestsellers, including *Intimacy and Solitude*, *Forgiveness and Other Acts of Love*, *Daily Acts of Love*, and *The Universal Heart*, and two novels, *Running Backwards Over Sand* and *Tasting Salt*. She is the mother of two teenagers, and a regular contributor to radio and newspapers.

www.stephaniedowrick.com

Listen to the teachings
of your heart.
At the end of each day,
find something to be
thankful for.
Give thanks.
Sleep in peace.